The Owl and the Pussy Cat

EDWARD LEAR · PAUL GALDONE

CLARION BOOKS
NEW YORK

Clarion Books • a Houghton Mifflin Company imprint • 215 Park Avenue South, New York, NY 10003 • Text copyright © 1987 by The Estate of Paul Galdone • All rights reserved. Printed in Mexico • For information about permission to reproduce selections from this book, write to Permissions, Houghton Mifflin Company, 215 Park Avenue South, New York, NY 10003. • For information about this and other Houghton Mifflin trade and reference books and multimedia products, visit The Bookstore at Houghton Mifflin on the World Wide Web at (http://www.hmco.com/trade/).

Library of Congress Cataloging-in-Publication Data
Lear, Edward, 1812–1888. The owl and the pussy-cat.
Summary: After a courtship voyage of a year and a day, Owl and Pussy finally buy a ring from Piggy and are blissfully married. 1. Children's poetry, English. [1. Nonsense verses. 2. Animals—Poetry. 3. English poetry] I. Galdone, Paul, ill. II. Title. PR4879.L209 1987b 821'.8 86 -17034
ISBN 0-89919-505-9

RDT 15 14 13 12 11

The Owl and the Pussy-cat went to sea

In a beautiful pea-green boat,

They took some honey,
and plenty of money,
Wrapped up in a five-pound note.

The Owl looked up
to the stars above,

And sang to a small guitar,

"O lovely Pussy! O Pussy, my love,
What a beautiful Pussy you are,

You are,
You are!
What a beautiful Pussy you are!"

Pussy said to the Owl,
"You elegant fowl!
How charmingly sweet you sing!

O let us be married!
too long we have tarried:

But what shall we do for a ring?"

They sailed away,
for a year and a day,
To the land where
the Bong-tree grows

And there in a wood
a Piggy-wig stood,

With a ring at the end of his nose,
His nose,
His nose,
With a ring at the end of his nose.

"Dear Pig, are you willing
to sell for one shilling

Your ring?"
Said the Piggy, "I will."

So they took it away,
and were married next day

By the Turkey who
lives on the hill.

They dined on mince,
and slices of quince,

Which they ate
with a runcible spoon;

And hand in hand,
on the edge of the sand,
They danced by the light of
the moon,

The moon, the moon,

They danced by the light of
the moon.